m

15

Raintree • Chicago, Illinois

PLAYGROUND SURVIVAL

by Peggy Burns

Illustrated by Deborah Allwright

© 2005 Raintree
Published by Raintree, a division of Reed Elsevier Inc.
Chicago, Illinois

Customer Service 888-363-4266

Visit our website at www.raintreelibrary.com

Illustrated by Deborah Allwright
Packaged by Ticktock Media Ltd.
Designed by Robert Walster, BigBlu Design
Printed and bound in China, by South China Printing

09 08 07 06 05
10 9 8 7 6 5 4 3 2 1

Library of Congress Cataloging-in-Publication Data
Burns, Peggy, 1941-
   Playground survival / Peggy Burns.
      p. cm. -- (Kids' guides)
   Includes bibliographical references and index.
   Contents: Friend troubles -- Being different -- School bullies -- Talking it through -- What would you do?
   ISBN 1-4109-0572-1 (lib. bdg.)
 1. Child psychology--Juvenile literature. 2. Interpersonal relations in children--Juvenile literature. 3. Bullying--Juvenile literature.
 [1. Interpersonal relations. 2. Self-esteem. 3. Bullying.] I. Title. II. Series: Kids' guides (Chicago, Ill.)
   HQ772.5.B874 2005
   302.3'4--dc22

                              2003021987

Some words are shown in bold, **like this.** You can find out what they mean by looking in the glossary.

CONTENTS

INTRODUCTION

Going to school can be lots of fun. There are so many exciting things to do: games to play, interesting things to learn, new friends to make. But great as school can be, things don't always run smoothly. It is good to have friends to play with. But even best friends can become **jealous,** start teasing each other, or say hurtful things.

Not everyone finds it easy to make friends. Maybe it seems like other children do not want to play with you. It could be because you are **shy** or because you are different from them in some way. They might not know you, yet they have made up their minds not to like you. This can make you feel unhappy and lonely.

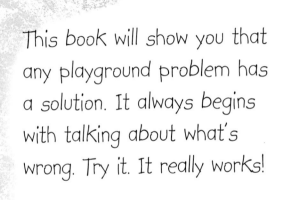

This book will show you that any playground problem has a solution. It always begins with talking about what's wrong. Try it. It really works!

Let's Talk About...
FRIEND TROUBLES

It is great to have friends. You always have someone to talk to, play with, and share secrets with. Friends are there for the good times, and help each other through the bad times, but even best friends **quarrel.** You both may say unkind things. Before you know it, you aren't talking to each other at all.

BUT WHY ME?

Everyone gets along with some people more than others. Friends may argue, and they may even fight. But if someone is nasty to you a lot of the time, he or she is not a true friend.

That's not fair.

You cheated.

WHY DO I FEEL LIKE THIS?

If you fight with a friend, you might be very angry at first. But after a while, you start to feel unhappy and lonely. Things just aren't the same without your friend!

Children everywhere have disagreements from time to time. Making up can be difficult, especially if you both think the other person is wrong! It helps to:
● Smile at your friend to show you are not still angry.
● Say you are sorry.
● Talk about it, then move on to becoming friends again.

LOOK AT IT ANOTHER WAY

If you are in a fight, you are probably thinking about your own feelings. But your friend is probably just as upset. Saying sorry is never easy, but being friends again is well worth it!

Let's Talk About...
BEING DIFFERENT

The world would be boring if all people were the same. No two people in the world are exactly alike. Even identical twins have different interests and talents. You may be confident or **shy,** tall or short, black or white.

Some people turn against others simply because they are different. This is called **prejudice.**

You can play but not your friend.

Then I won't play thanks!

He's prejudiced.

BUT WHY ME?

It is very unfair when people make up their minds that they don't like you before they know you. You can't help how other people think. But you can decide that their prejudice is not going to hurt you.

Prejudiced people dislike someone for no good reason. They may judge a person before they know them. They may think they are better than you. They may call you mean names or refuse to be friends with you.

WHY DO I FEEL LIKE THIS?

If someone is making you feel unwanted, ugly, or unimportant, they are in the wrong, not you. If they weren't being nasty to you, you wouldn't be feeling this way.

Those girls are rude... but that's their problem.

LOOK AT IT ANOTHER WAY

People usually think the same things as their parents and family. They might be prejudiced because of the way they were brought up. Their views can be changed.

Being treated unfairly makes you feel angry, sad, and hurt, but remember:

● The other person is the one with a problem, not you.

● Walk away rather than let the person see that you are upset.

● You are important and special.

● Never believe the things prejudiced people say about you.

Let's Talk About...
SCHOOL BULLIES

Being bullied is the worst thing to deal with on the playground. A bully might hit you, pull your hair, or take your things. He or she might spread **rumors** about you, or say nasty things to you. They might ignore you and get others to stop talking to you.

WHY DO I FEEL LIKE THIS?

Being bullied is very upsetting. Bullies can make you feel lonely, sad, angry, or scared.

Why won't they leave me alone?

BUT WHY ME?

People are bullied because the bully has a problem. The bully may say it is because you are small or tall, thin or fat, poor or rich. It is really about the bully looking for ways to hurt someone. It's not about you!

Sometimes people who are bullied believe what the bully says and feel bad about themselves. This makes the bully feel that he or she has won.

I must be doing something wrong.

If you are bullied, it is NOT your fault. It is the bully's fault. So remember:

- You are not to blame.
- You do not deserve to be picked on for any reason.
- All bullying is wrong.
- Telling an adult is the only way to stop a bully.

I've got to tell someone.

LOOK AT IT ANOTHER WAY

Bullies are often unhappy deep down inside. They may be **jealous** of the people they bully. Or they may have been bullied themselves. Whatever the reason, bullies have to be stopped. But they may need help, too.

True Stories

THREE'S A CROWD

Hi there. I'm Ellie. Sheema has been my best friend for a long time. We started school on the same day! Recently a new family moved onto our street, and I made friends with Hannah.

I hate playing on my own.

Hannah joined our class. Sheema, Hannah, and I all started playing together. But then they started to leave me out. I didn't know why.

Then someone told me that Sheema was spreading a **rumor** about me. She told everyone my dad left home because he doesn't love me or my mom anymore. Everyone thinks it's true!

I'm really upset with Sheema. She knows my dad has a job out of town. But he's coming home soon!

THREE'S A CROWD

Talking It Through

It helps to talk to someone...

A BROTHER

Ellie's brother Luke cannot understand why Ellie's best friend would hurt her like that. He tells Ellie to talk to Sheema to find out why she has made up the story.

A PARENT

Ellie writes to her dad and tells him what has happened. He is very upset! He writes back and tells Ellie that she should take his letter to school and show it to her friends.

A PARENT

Ellie's mom wonders what could have made Sheema spread such a **rumor.** She says Sheema must have her reasons. She is going to talk to Sheema's mom about what happened.

FORWARD STEPS

● **TALK**
Don't keep problems bottled up inside you.

● **SHARE**
You can be friends with more than one person.

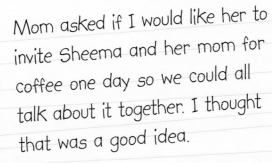

Mom asked if I would like her to invite Sheema and her mom for coffee one day so we could all talk about it together. I thought that was a good idea.

Sheema turned red and said she was **jealous** when I'd become friends with Hannah. She didn't want to share her best friend with anyone. She told lies about me, hoping that Hannah wouldn't want me as a friend any more. She was really **ashamed** of what she'd done. She said she was sorry. Then she told the kids at school the truth, which must have been very hard. I took Dad's letter to school with a photo of him working on his building site. He'd sent candy, too, which I shared with my class!

HE'S A WEIRDO

Hi, my name is Robert. I just started at a new school. I was nervous to go, because I have **epilepsy.** I take medicine to control it, but I do sometimes have **seizures.** The teacher told the class about it, though, so I thought everything would be fine.

I don't remember a thing.

I quickly got to know people and made friends with Luke. Then one day I had an attack in the playground. My attacks don't last long, but my mom says they are frightening to watch. I fall down and start shaking.

After that, people didn't want to be friends with me anymore. Luke said I was freaky. And I thought he was my friend! Why are they afraid of me? I'm no weirdo.

HE'S A WEIRDO
Talking It Through

It helps to talk to someone...

A SISTER

Robert's big sister, Kate, reminds him that thousands of people have **epilepsy.** She says he should explain to the kids at school about epilepsy. There's nothing freaky about having an illness.

A PARENT

Robert's dad says he should feel good about himself. He is coping very well with having epilepsy. He says he will go to Robert's school and talk with his teacher.

A TEACHER

Mr. Harris has already told the class about Robert's illness. He realizes now that they need to know more. He tells Robert not to worry, he will have a class discussion about it.

FORWARD STEPS

- **TELL YOUR TEACHER**
It is important for teachers to know if you have an illness. They can help the other kids understand.

- **YOU'RE OKAY**
Having an illness or disability of any kind does not make anyone a weirdo!

I was glad I'd told my family what happened. Dad went and talked to Mr. Harris. That same day, Mr. Harris told the class that I might have a **seizure** again. He said that it might be a bit upsetting, but there was nothing freaky about having epilepsy. There was nothing to be scared of. We all talked about it, so everyone could learn what it was like to have epilepsy. He made it clear that nobody should be picked on because of having an illness.

At playtime Luke said he was sorry for calling me names. We're best friends now. When I had another seizure last week, Luke took charge. He was a big help!

Are you okay now?

Yes. Thanks, Luke.

True Stories

THE SCHOOL BULLY

Hello, my name is Andreas. My dad is American, and my mom was Italian. They **divorced** when I was little, and I lived with my mom in Italy. But last spring she died. That was horrible. Then I came to live with my dad in the United States. I am learning to speak English, but I am not very good at it yet. I go to the local elementary school, but I don't like it because of Dwayne and his friends.

Oh, no! Here they come again.

Tell anyone and we will get you!

They make fun of my Italian **accent,** trip me, and take my things. The other day, Dwayne grabbed my gym shirt and stuffed it down the toilet. He said that if I tell anyone, they will beat me up.

I'm too scared to go to school, so I have told my dad I feel sick. I know he doesn't believe me. I don't know what to do.

THE SCHOOL BULLY

Talking It Through

It helps to talk to someone...

A FRIEND

Josh sits next to Andreas at school, and he has seen the way that Dwayne and his gang are bullying him. He tells Andreas he should talk to a grown-up about it.

A PARENT

Andreas's dad is pleased he's talked to him. He tells him that grown-ups can help with problems, but only if they are told about them. He says he'll go to school to talk to Andreas's teacher.

A TEACHER

Miss Rees is sad to hear that Andreas is being bullied. She tells him not to be scared of Dwayne anymore. She is going to make sure that the bullying stops for good.

FORWARD STEPS

● **BE STRONG**
Don't allow *bullies* to rule your life.

● **TELL SOMEONE**
If you are *being bullied*, you should tell a grown-up you can trust. Bullies *must be made* to stop hurting you, and they need help, too.

I wasn't going to be bullied by anyone ever again.

So you know how horrible it feels, Dwayne.

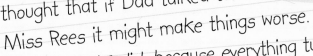
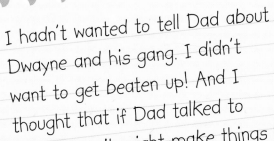

I hadn't wanted to tell Dad about Dwayne and his gang. I didn't want to get beaten up! And I thought that if Dad talked to Miss Rees it might make things worse. But I'm glad I did, because everything turned out fine. In class we talked about why people bully, and how people who are bullied feel. Everybody joined in. Dwayne told us he was bullied at his last school. He said that when he came here he didn't want to be bullied any more. He turned into a bully instead. But he promised us he'd stop.

Now I enjoy school. I'm not scared any more. Dwayne leaves me alone, and my English is getting better all the time.

23

True Stories
GREEN-EYED MONSTER

Hi there, I'm Daisy. Not long ago, we moved to a new house, and I started going to a new school. Ruth sits next to me in class. Last week she invited me to her birthday party. I wanted to go, but I had no money for a present or a card, because my dad's out of work right now.

I hope she likes it.

Mom said I should make Ruth a card. So I painted a picture of a flower and wrote "Happy Birthday, Ruth!" on it.

Look, Mom, another Barbie!

At the party I realized that Ruth's parents are rich. I was **embarrassed** to give Ruth my homemade card! Everyone else had brought her a present. The best one was a Barbie with long shiny hair and lots of clothes. Suddenly, I hated Ruth for having everything she wants. Why do I have to be poor?

GREEN-EYED MONSTER

Talking It Through

It helps to talk to someone...

A GRANDPARENT

Daisy's grandad says he understands how she feels. He tells her to be **patient** for a while longer. He is sure that her dad will get a job soon. After that, things should get better.

A SISTER

Daisy's sister Alison tells her not to turn into a "green-eyed monster." She says that is a name for **jealous** people. It isn't right to dislike someone just because they've got nice things.

A FRIEND

Her friend, Ruth, tells Daisy that what a person is like inside is more important than having money. She thinks it is better to be nice than rich. And she says Daisy is very nice!

FORWARD STEPS

● BE POSITIVE

Try not to be jealous when friends have things that your parents can't afford. Envy can take over your thoughts if you let it!

● BE NICE

Even if you are poor, you can make sure that you are a nice person.

We can't always have everything we want.

We should be thankful for what we have!

On the next school day, Ruth thanked me for the birthday card. She said it was the nicest one, because I'd made it just for her! I stopped feeling **ashamed** that it was homemade.

After the party I'd felt very jealous of Ruth. It didn't seem fair that she had four Barbies when I didn't even have one! But talking about it helped a lot. I know now that I was wrong to judge Ruth because her family is rich. It's more important that Ruth and I are both nice people.

And yesterday, my dad had an **interview.** I hope he gets the job!

Quiz

WHAT WOULD YOU DO?

1. What would you do if someone at school was telling lies and spreading **rumors** about you, like Ellie?

a) Decide that you will never speak to that person again.

b) Start spreading a rumor about the person, to get even.

c) Try to find out why he or she would want to make others believe something that isn't true.

d) Don't say anything about it, and wait for everyone to forget the rumor.

2. What would you do if, like Robert, you had an illness that made you seem different, and people were calling you names?

a) Make sure that your friends understand about your illness.

b) Stay in the background and hope that the teasing will stop.

c) Think up a few bad names that you can call them.

d) Wait for them to get tired of picking on you.

3. What would you do if, like Andreas, you were being bullied?

a) Run away.

b) Keep quiet about it, hoping the bully will leave you alone and pick on someone else.

c) Talk to a grown-up about it.

d) Learn to fight back.

4. What would you do if, like Daisy, you felt **jealous** of a friend whose parents could afford to give her whatever she wants?

a) Decide that all rich people are snobs.

b) Get angry with your own parents for being poor.

c) Feel sorry for yourself.

d) Decide that nobody deserves to be disliked for being rich or poor.

Answers

1. c) There are always reasons why people act the way they do. It is important to talk things over and find out why they are telling lies about you. Then you can find a solution to the problem.

2. a) People need to know how your illness affects you!

3. c) Always tell a grown-up if you are being bullied. Bullies need to be stopped. And they may need help, too.

4. d) None of us can choose the family we are born into, but we should all be thankful for the one we have.

Glossary

accent   way a person pronounces words

ashamed   feeling upset because of the way you have behaved

disability   handicap that makes someone unable to do something

divorced   when a marriage is legally ended

embarrassed   when someone feels self-conscious and awkward

epilepsy   disease that causes someone to have fits

interview   talk between an employer and a person looking for work to find out whether he or she is right for a job

jealousy or jealous   wanting to be like someone else or have something he or she has

patient   remain calm in difficult situations

prejudice   judge another person before knowing them or knowing all the facts

rumor   story that is passed around which may not be true

quarrel   argue or disagree

seizure   sudden fit, or an attack of illness

shy   not sure of oneself, not outgoing

More Books to Read

Clements, Andrew. **Jake Drake, Bully Buster.** New York: Simon & Schuster, 2001.

Kline, Suzy. **Molly Gets Mad.** New York: Putnam, 2001.

Levete, Sarah. **Being Jealous.** Brookfield, Conn.: Millbrook, 1999.

McCain, Becky R. **Nobody Knew What to Do: A Story About Bullying.** Morton Grove, Ill.: Whitman, 2001.

Powell, Jillian. **Bullying.** Chicago: Raintree, 1999.

Waters, Jennifer. **Be a Good Friend!** Minneapolis: Compass Point, 2002.

Index